Table of Contents

INTRODUCTION

Basecamp is an online project management and team communication software that helps businesses get organized. It centralizes teams, tools, files, and messages, allowing users to collaborate easily and effectively.

Built-in automation, to-do lists, shared calendars, and client access enables teams to boost productivity with increased transparency. For teams looking for different capabilities or more affordability, several Basecamp alternatives are readily available.

Basecamp is a work management and collaboration tool that helps you organize projects and communications. It's benefits are clear: it keeps you and your work organized, making it clear what tasks are due and gathering all the information you need to execute on them; it brings everyone in your team and company onto the same page, allowing you to communicate more efficiently in a single place; and it allows you to maintain control over projects while easily sharing specific information and deliverables with clients.

Team communications are often the component that can sink a project if they're not handled well. Back and forth emails, time-consuming status meetings, and inefficient task follow up are all reasons companies turn to project management software like the Basecamp app.

The world of project management has evolved along with the technology we use, and today's applications for task management are much more efficient than using whiteboards or sticky notes.

Basecamp project management software offers tools that you won't find in some of its competitors. They've chosen to ditch the Kanban boards and instead forge an original path that includes tools like message boards, hill charts, and check-in questions.

They must be doing something right because the Basecamp project management tool has grown steadily in the number of users, reaching $3 million account signups in 2019.

Lack of coordination within a team is cited by 97% of executives and employees as making a big impact on task or project outcome. In our Basecamp project management review, we found that the main driver behind the app is to improve team communication.

Today, businesses and teams are using project management to help improve the chances of achieving their desired result. PM standards exist to help project managers plan work, assign tasks, lead teams, track progress, monitor status, and communicate updates. Still, every company or team has a different and preferred way of getting work done. As a result, the PM software market is full of choices, including online tools. One of the most effective online project management tools is Basecamp.

Basecamp is a tool that works on the philosophy of "real-time communication" and serves the proverb of "being on the same page" almost literally. With features of having to-do lists, calendars, file sharing capabilities, it avoids the traditional project management ways and helps users incorporate the new style of project management tasks. With the software, teams can easily keep track of the priorities and items which are actionable. The software is such that it allows the user to access it not only through the browser but also through the phone. All in one place, it ensures that the user doesn't have to go anywhere else for managing the product by not only organizing but also helping you and your team to collaborate even more effectively.

With an upgraded one also gets an additional feature that helps ease the aspect of dealing with clients. With the addition of your client into space and allowing them to have a limited view of what's in place makes them also feel like an integral part of the work and provides a sense of belief on us because of the pure transparency, we can provide through this tool to the clients. Again, this a feeling of keeping the clients "on the same page".

People who have used Basecamp have a specific reason of why they love Basecamp, and some of the key features which users have talked about in the reviews are, one can set or comment or even assign tasks as granular as to a specific file and once the comments are pushed in Basecamp automatically notifies to the owner about the comment. Now one would eventually think that all these notifications would be sent through mails as there will be quite a back and forth of the changes but wait! The conversation happens over in a skype chat or even over the phone. It makes you feel like you are chatting about your work, and that's what people say makes it even interesting.

WHAT IS BASECAMP USED FOR?

Basecamp is mainly used to:

- Manage multiple projects and tasks
- Communicate with your entire team or specific members
- Create and track project progress and schedules
- Store project-related documents
- Basecamp is a suitable solution for both startups and large corporations. And if you have remote team members, they can just hop on the app and start collaborating too.

4 KEY FEATURES OF BASECAMP

Let's check out what makes Basecamp an excellent communication and project management tool:

1. To-do lists

Complicated problems don't always warrant complex solutions. Sometimes all you need is something simple, like a to-do list. To-do lists form the backbone of

Basecamp. It helps you break down large, complicated projects into smaller tasks. You can then assign tasks to your team members and set deadlines.

Completed a task? Just tick it off to mark it as complete, just like checking off items on your grocery list.

Basecamp also lets you:

- Archive to-dos for future reference
- Assign multiple people to a specific task list
- Add notes, images, or files to a list

2. Hill charts

When it comes to flying, Batman certainly doesn't rank high up on the list. But when it comes to planning, he's definitely number 1. And that's because he always takes an eagle's-eye view of the situation to plan efficiently. Similarly, you need to see the bigger picture to ensure your project runs smoothly. Basecamp's hill charts help you do just that.

In the hill chart, you can group tasks (aka your to-dos) into two phases: ideation (uphill) and execution (downhill). Team members can manually drag and drop to-do lists across the hill based on their progress. And with a glance at the hill chart, you can tell how things are moving.

3. Message boards

Want to announce a project update? Or maybe plan a virtual party with your remote team? Use Basecamp's message boards to get the message across. Message boards let you organize conversations about a specific topic on a single page. Based on your post type, you can categorize it as announcements, questions, pitches, and more.

It also allows you to:

- Sort posts alphabetically, by date, and the latest comment
- Embed images into your message
- Customize who gets notified about the post

4. A powerful quick search feature

A quick search feature might not sound really cool until you think about Google's net worth today. And sometimes, you're just low on the energy juice and need a tool that can quickly pull up data for you.

With Basecamp's quick search feature, you can effortlessly search for particular terms, messages, and files. It also lets you narrow down results with filters for to-dos, comments, client emails, and more. Want to share a relevant result with your project team? Hit the copy button on the result to grab a link that you can share with your teammates.

6 MAJOR LIMITATIONS OF BASECAMP PROJECT MANAGEMENT (WITH SOLUTIONS)

Wouldn't it be amazing to have a genie that grants all your wishes?

You could ask for collaboration software that solves e-v-e-r-y-t-h-i-n-g (*wink* *wink*).

Unfortunately, Basecamp isn't that project management and collaboration tool.

Here are six significant limitations of Basecamp:

- Limited project views
- No task priorities
- Limited progress tracking functionality
- No native time tracking features
- No advanced customization options
- Expensive pricing plans

1. Limited project views

You going to stay relevant to the times you're in, right? You can use a Kanban board or Gantt chart in the modern project management realm to manage schedules and get better project results. But it looks like Basecamp didn't receive the memo.

It's been 15+ years, and the tool still uses to-do lists to manage projects. You'll have to rely on a third-party integration to use Gantt charts, Kanban boards, and other project management features. But why go for Basecamp and its expensive integrations when you can have it all with ClickUp?

ClickUp is one of the world's highest-rated productivity and project management apps, used by super-productive teams in small and large companies. Unlike Basecamp,

ClickUp doesn't restrict you to to-do lists. It offers a wide variety of project management features, suitable for teams of all sizes. For starters, ClickUp makes project organization a breeze with its easy-to-use Hierarchy Structure and Simple Layout.

And here's the main course:

- ClickUp solution: flexible project views
- Looking at things from different perspectives is essential, especially when your eye is on better project results.

And that's why ClickUp gives you a host of different Workspace views to choose from, like:

- List view: see tasks as a simple List and quickly group, sort, and filter them
- Box view: helps make informed decisions about who you can assign tasks to
- Calendar view: great for project planning and resource management
- Gantt Chart view: track how your project is progressing in real-time
- Activity view: get a summarized view of your team's activities
- Mind Maps view: map out project plans using existing tasks or create a free-form Mind Map
- Timeline view: create project schedules and roadmaps in a snap

- Board view: move projects through a custom agile workflow
- Workload view: visualize your team's capacity and manage workloads

2. No task priorities

Basecamp's to-do list lets you create tasks for your project. However, various tasks will have different priorities. Sorta like how cheese is more important than garlic when cooking lasagna. Unfortunately, Basecamp doesn't let you prioritize tasks. Team members could end up spending time on a low-priority task instead of an urgent one, which could derail your entire project.

ClickUp solution #1: Task Priorities

When learning something, you might use highlighters to mark important words.

ClickUp makes use of something like that. It gives you four color-coded flags to indicate task priority:

- Urgent (red)
- High (yellow)
- Normal (blue)
- Low (grey)

With a quick look at your tasks, you'll know what needs urgent attention and what can wait for later.

3. Limited progress tracking functionality

Remember Basecamp's hill chart? Well, it has a major problem. And we aren't talking about the manual effort required to update it each time. The real issue here is that you could end up with inaccurate data as each member could feel differently about the current progress. For example, someone might feel that 50% of the task is complete and update the chart accordingly when only 30% has been actually completed.

If you don't want your entire project to tumble downhill, you need a project management tool that lets you track the progress of multiple projects accurately. You need ClickUp.

ClickUp solution #1: Custom Statuses

Every project has unique stages. For example, a software development project may need planning, testing, and deployment phases. On the other hand, a sales project may need stages like prospecting, negotiation, etc. With Custom Statuses, you can track the progress of each phase the way you want to. You can create a customized workflow that suits both your team and project.

ClickUp solution #2: Dashboards

Project management is all about seeing the bigger picture.

That's why ClickUp's Dashboards give you a high-level overview of everything that's going on in your Workspace. It's the best way to monitor project progress and identify bottlenecks.

You can also add Sprint widgets like Burnups charts, Burndown charts, Cumulative Flow diagrams, and

Velocity charts to analyze your project progress in real-time.

4. No native time tracking features

Tracking project time is essential to bill your clients accurately and gain insights into your team's productivity. Unfortunately, Basecamp doesn't have any native time tracking features. If you want to track the time spent on tasks, you'll have to go for a Basecamp integration.

ClickUp solution #1: Native Time Tracking

With ClickUp's built-in global timer, you won't have to leave the app or use a third-party app to track time. Just start and stop the timer for a relevant task from any device you're logged in. ClickUp will automatically track your hours down to the second. Already have a favorite time tracking app?

No worries. ClickUp integrates with several time trackers like Time Doctor, Everhour, and Clockify for added functionality. And no, you won't have to pay for these integrations. ClickUp's Free Forever Plan comes with 50+ native integrations! Take notes, Basecamp.

ClickUp solution #2: Time Tracking Widgets

Straight off the bat, ClickUp offers you several Time Tracking Widgets that you can add to your Dashboard.

You get Widgets like:

- Time Reporting: visualize all your time entries with different filters
- Billable Report: see only the billable project time
- Time Estimated: quickly view time as a team resource for managing projects
- Time Tracked: know how much time each team member has tracked
- Timesheet: see time tracked for a given week, month, or any custom range

This way, you won't have to spend time worrying about where all the time went!

5. No advanced customization options

While Basecamp seems like an iron-clad tool, it's got a pretty big chink in its armor.

What do we mean?

Since Basecamp's pretty simple, it doesn't offer many customization options.

However, different departments need to customize their projects and workflows to reflect their needs accurately. Unfortunately, Basecamp doesn't offer much in this department.

ClickUp solution: intuitively customizable

Remember Custom Statuses in ClickUp?

Well, that's not the only thing you can customize.

Here's a quick look at what else you can customize in ClickUp:

- Custom Fields: add additional data to your projects to manage them the way you want
- Custom Roles: create a well-organized workflow with specific user roles
- Custom Notifications: choose how and when you receive notifications from ClickUp

6. Expensive pricing plans

Basecamp's paid plan costs $99/month.

The problem?

Not only is it expensive but it's also a flat rate. You'll have to pay the same amount even if your team has four members or 40 members.

Sometimes simplicity comes at a cost. On top of that, Basecamp's free personal plan only lets you manage three projects! ClickUp solution: flexible pricing plans

ClickUp's Free Forever Plan is enough to kick Basecamp out of the water. You get unlimited projects, unlimited users, and a wide variety of awesome features for free.

And instead of a flat fee, ClickUp's paid plans start as low as $5/month per user with features like unlimited file storage. As the pricing is on a per-user basis, you get your money's worth.

But that's not all.

Here are even more reasons why ClickUp is the ultimate Basecamp alternative:

- Docs: create onboarding documents, wikis, and user guides right inside ClickUp
- Reminders: manage personal projects with personal Due Dates and Reminders
- Collaboration Detection: know when someone views or edits the same task or document as you
- Clip: a native screen recording feature that eliminates the need for third-party software like Loom.

Time to Break Camp

Sure, Basecamp is simple and has some decent project management and team collaboration features.

But is it a fantastic, all-in-one project management solution?

Nope.

A robust project management app like ClickUp offers you advanced functionality and a lot more flexibility. From features like recurring tasks and 100+ Automations to task Dependencies, ClickUp is the ultimate Basecamp alternative. Try ClickUp for free today to experience what the best project management software can do for you. No strings attached.

Below you'll find a collection of general principles we try to keep in mind at Basecamp when communicating with teammates, within departments, across the company, and with the public. They aren't requirements, but they serve to create boundaries and shared practices to draw upon when we do the one thing that affects everything else we do: communicate.

You can not not communicate. Not discussing the elephant in the room is communicating. Few things are as important to study, practice, and perfect as clear communication.

Real-time sometimes, asynchronous most of the time.

Internal communication based on long-form writing, rather than a verbal tradition of meetings, speaking, and chatting, leads to a welcomed reduction in meetings, video conferences, calls, or other real-time opportunities to interrupt and be interrupted.

Give meaningful discussions a meaningful amount of time to develop and unfold. Rushing to judgement, or demanding immediate responses, only serves to increase the odds of poor decision making.

Meetings are the last resort, not the first option.

Writing solidifies, chat dissolves. Substantial decisions start and end with an exchange of complete thoughts, not one-line-at-a-time jousts. If it's important, critical, or fundamental, write it up, don't chat it down.

Speaking only helps who's in the room, writing helps everyone. This includes people who couldn't make it, or future employees who join years from now.

If your words can be perceived in different ways, they'll be understood in the way which does the most harm.

Never expect or require someone to get back to you immediately unless it's a true emergency. The expectation of immediate response is toxic.

If you have to repeat yourself, you weren't clear enough the first time. However, if you're talking about something brand new, you may have to repeat yourself for years before you're heard. Pick your repeats wisely.

Poor communication creates more work.

Companies don't have communication problems, they have miscommunication problems. The smaller the company, group, or team, the fewer opportunities for miscommunication.

Five people in a room for an hour isn't a one hour meeting, it's a five hour meeting. Be mindful of the tradeoffs.

Be proactive about "wait, what?" questions by providing factual context and spatial context. Factual are the things people also need to know. Spatial is where the communication happens (for example, if it's about a specific to-do, discuss it right under the to-do, not somewhere else).

Communication shouldn't require schedule synchronization. Calendars have nothing to do with communication. Writing, rather than speaking or meeting, is independent of schedule and far more direct.

"Now" is often the wrong time to say what just popped into your head. It's better to let it filter it through the sieve of time. What's left is the part worth saying.

Ask yourself if others will feel compelled to rush their response if you rush your approach.

The end of the day has a way of convincing you what you've done is good, but the next morning has a way of telling you the truth. If you aren't sure, sleep on it before saying it.

If you want an answer, you have to ask a question. People typically have a lot to say, but they'll volunteer little. Automatic questions on a regular schedule help people practice sharing, writing, and communicating.

Occasionally pick random words, sentences, or paragraphs and hit delete. Did it matter?

Urgency is overrated, ASAP is poison.

If something's going to be difficult to hear or share, invite questions at the end. Ending without the invitation will lead to public silence but private conjecture. This is where rumors breed.

Where you put something, and what you call it, matters. When titling something, lead with the most important information. Keep in mind that many technical systems truncate long text or titles.

Write at the right time. Sharing something at 5pm may keep someone at work longer. You may have some spare time on a Sunday afternoon to write something, but putting it out there on Sunday may pull people back into work on the weekends. Early Monday morning communication may be buried by other things. There may not be a perfect time, but there's certainly a wrong time. Keep that in mind when you hit send.

Great news delivered on the heels of bad news makes both bits worse. The bad news feels like it's being buried, the good news feels like it's being injected to change the mood. Be honest with each by giving them adequate space.

Time is on your side, rushing makes conversations worse.

Communication is lossy, especially verbal communication. Every hearsay hop adds static and chips at fidelity. Whenever possible, communicate directly with those you're addressing rather than passing the message through intermediaries.

Ask if things are clear. Ask what you left out. Ask if there was anything someone was expecting that you didn't cover. Address the gaps before they widen with time.

Consider where you put things. The right communication in the wrong place might as well not exist at all. When someone relies on search to find something it's often because it wasn't where they expected something to be.

Communication often interrupts, so good communication is often about saying the right thing at the right time in the right way with the fewest side effects.

Communicating day-to-day

This section includes specific examples of how we apply our philosophy day-to-day across the company. Since communication often interrupts, valuing each other's time and attention is a critical consideration. Keeping people in the loop is important, but asking them to follow along with everything is a distraction. That's why we follow reliable, predictable methods to share the right kind of information at the right time in the right place.

Basic toolset

98% of our internal communication happens inside Basecamp. That means all company-wide discussions, social chatter, project-related work, sharing of ideas, internal debates, automatic check-ins, status updates, policy updates, and all official decisions and announcements all happen in Basecamp. A single centralized tool keeps everything together and creates a single source of truth for everyone across the company. We don't use email internally (we do externally), we don't use separate chat tools like Slack or Teams, and we rarely have in-person meetings. We do use Zoom or Skype for the occasional video conference between two or three people. And we occasionally discuss a pull request in GitHub.

Automatic daily: "What did you work on today?

Every workday at 16:30, Basecamp (the product) automatically asks every employee "What did you work on today?" Whatever people write up is shared with everyone in the company. Everyone's responses are displayed on a single page, grouped by date, so anyone who's curious about what's happening across the company can simply read from top to bottom. And if you have a question about anything, you can comment on anyone's "what did you work on today?" check-in to keep the conversation in context.

This routine is about loose accountability and strong reflection. Writing up what you did every day is a great way to think back about what you accomplished and how you spent your time.

Some people just jot down a few bullets. Others write multi-paragraph stories to share - and document - the thinking behind their work. There are no requirements here. We just ask everyone to write in their own style.

Automatic weekly: "What will you be working on this week?"

Every Monday morning, Basecamp automatically asks everyone "What will you be working on this week?" This is a chance for everyone to lay out the big picture of their week. It's not about regurgitating individual tasks, or diving headlong into the minutia of the week. It's generally just your 10,000 foot view of the week ahead. The big picture items, the general themes. It sets your mind up for the work ahead, and, collectively, it gives everyone a good sense of what's happening across the company this week.

Automatic occasionally: "Social questions"

Every few weeks, or once a month, Basecamp will automatically ask everyone a social-style question. "What books are you reading?" Or "Try anything new lately?" Or "Anything inspire you lately?" Or "Seen any great design recently?" Or "What did you do this weekend?" These entirely optional questions are meant to shake loose some stuff that you'd love to share with everyone else, but you hadn't had an opportunity to do so. This kind of internal communication helps grease the social gears. This is especially useful for remote teams, like ours. When we know each other a little better, we work a little better together.

Reflect every 6 weeks: Heartbeats

Heartbeats summarize the last ~6-weeks of work for a given team, department, or individual (if that person is a department of one). They're written by the lead of the group, and they're meant for everyone in the company to read. They summarize the big picture accomplishments, they detail the little things that mattered, and they generally highlight the importance of the work. They'll also shine a light on challenges and difficulties along the way. They're a good reminder that it's not all sunshine all the time. On balance, Heartbeats are wonderful to write, fun to read, and they help everyone - including those not directly involved with the work - reflect on jobs well done and progress well made.

Project every 6 weeks: Kickoffs

Kickoffs are essentially the opposites of Heartbeats. Rather than reflect, they project. They're all about what the team plans on taking on over the next 6 weeks. Projects, initiatives, revamps, whatever it might be, if it's on the slate, it gets summarized in the Kickoff. While Kickoffs detail specific work for a specific group, they're also meant for full-company consumption. Like Heartbeats, they're written by the team lead. Kickoffs are broad in scope, so they don't cover all the details in the work ahead - the teams doing the work are the ones that wade into those weeds. We don't want to overwhelm everyone with details that don't matter. If anyone's curious about something included in a Kickoff, they're free to post a comment and ask a question.

Whenever relevant: Announcements

Occasionally we update an internal policy. Something about vacation time, or a new benefit, or reiterating that 40 hour weeks means 40 hour weeks. When we have something to announce company-wide, we don't send an email. Email is decentralized and there's no permanent record in a permanent place everyone can see. Instead, we post it either to the Basecamp HQ message board or as a comment on an existing policy document stored in Basecamp. This means everyone sees the same thing, everyone hears the same thing, and everyone knows the same thing - including future employees who are yet to join Basecamp. We now have a shared truth.

Day-to-day project work: In context

Effective communication requires context. Saying the right thing in the wrong place, or without proper detail, leads to double work and messages being missed. That's why we spin up a separate Basecamp project for every project we work on. Everything related to that project is communicated inside that project. All the tasks, all the discussions, all the documents, all the debates, and all the decisions happen inside those walls. Everyone who needs access, has access. Every Basecamp project is a capsule of everything someone needs to know about that work project.

Further, we take spatial context seriously. If we're discussing a specific task, we discuss it in the comment section below the task itself. If we're talking about a specific document, we discuss it in the comments attached to the document. Communications stay attached to the thing we're discussing. This provides the full story in one reliable place. The alternative is terrible - communication detached from the original source material, discussions all over the place, fragmented conversations missing entire chunks of time and detail, etc. Basecamp's "everything is commentable" feature is what makes this possible for us.

Basecamp is widely used in organizations looking into the aspect of the ways it helps in streamlining the business. There 3 ways in which Basecamp is one of the most reached out tools, and hence below are the pointers on why we use Basecamp.

We have all the communication in one place: For example, let say one person in the team needs to share the dashboard he has been working on for quite a long to get inputs and feedbacks. So instead of sending a mail and then getting a reply back in hundreds of emails, he can utilize Basecamp to upload the Dashboard file, and the corresponding stakeholders get notified, and they are ready to view that along with having the capability to leave a comment on the work. What's more useful for the person who has built the dashboard is that he would no longer have to scorch through 100s of emails and also have the capability to search for a pointer in the list of comments he would eventually receive!

Basecamp doesn't force you to use only the tools it asks to but instead adapts to the tools which already is in place with you and can link with those tools you already have. For example, using Basecamp, you can easily configure your Google Drive, and this will enable you just to make changes in the Google drive only, and that's it! No more additional changes would be required specifically for documents going into Basecamp. From a schedule perspective, it easily integrates with Google Calendar, iCal!

Work with one free Basecamp: For a team size that involves few people and managing less project, one can avail the free Basecamp and get used to the feature even before committing getting something big of an investment!

WHO IS BASECAMP FOR?

Basecamp is the perfect tool for collaborative teams looking to track multiple projects and tasks, store and share team documents, and increase communication regarding task progress. This system works best as a collaboration tool for staff projects that do not require any budget planning, invoicing, or time tracking.

I've used Basecamp to track projects requiring lots of creative input, such as developing social media marketing campaigns, organizing event promotions, graphic design projects, and even company rebranding efforts. It's mainly a collaboration and planning tool best for internal team projects.

FEATURES OF BASECAMP

The above section mentions about the different points on why we use Basecamp, and these pointers are based on the features.

some of the key set of features are:

1. List of to-do having multiple levels and features: Basecamp well understands the crux of getting a project done, and thus, this feature of having a multi-level list allows you to add a sub-category to

a category and assign to a team member and tag a note along!

2. Co-workers Collaboration: With a new project or maybe even an existing one, the team members can be invited to collaborate on the project. There are different levels of access so that efficient control is still intact even with many people "collaborating".

3. Restriction on timing for notification: For you to enjoy your personal life, one can switch off the notifications for "outside work hours".

4. Chat real time: The chat tool is known as "Campfires" is a collaboration tool with chat capability to talk about work-related things and have a virtual time together!

5. Work on the go: As per your availability, Basecamp provides you with the flexibility to work out of anywhere you like, phone, tablet, or laptop. Super handy! Isn't it?

6. Basecamp provides you with the capability to hold discussions as well within its suite. Discussion topics can be created and made available to the team members to put forward their viewpoint, making it an efficient method of brainstorming!

7. Project Calendar: The project calendar is easy to manage out of Basecamp and sync up with the Google Calendar or iCal or Outlook calendar, making you super-efficient in terms of track!

So here we formally put down the advantages:

1. A single place to store files and documents.
2. Transparent pricing system.
3. Customizable on/off notification option.
4. Efficient communication system.
5. Transparency in terms of client accessibility.
6. Easy creation of hill charts.
7. Easy integration with existing tools!

Basecamp's features

Basecamp keeps it simple in the features department and goes for a more collaboratively based approach. It offers task management, commenting, file sharing, and scheduling features that'll help you keep internal projects on track.

Management and planning features:

Task prioritization and scheduler: Basecamp offers a task list system that allows you to tag relevant users, comment on task progress, and share project resources (documents, graphics, charts, etc.).

Documentation features:

- Document storage: Every project on Basecamp has a docs and files section where you can upload images, documents, and spreadsheets from your local computer as well as documents from your Google office suite.

Collaboration features:

- File sharing: Each Basecamp project and task has a file uploading and sharing system so you can quickly share resources with the rest of your team.
- Communication: Not only does each task in Basecamp have a comment section and messaging platform so you can communicate with your team, but Basecamp also sends email notifications whenever you're away from the app. That way, you'll never miss a task update or completion.

Budgeting features

Basecamp doesn't offer any financial management features such as budgeting, expenses, or invoicing.

BASECAMP PRICING GUIDE FOR 2022

If you're thinking about updating your work management software, you've probably already been tasked with often fruitless searches for things like "Basecamp pricing" or "this is the ONLY solution for team projects". Next, you're trying to see which tools have free trials so you can get a sense of worthwhile products before you commit to a price ticket.

While the feature offerings and potential for productivity surely will expand with a paid plan, how can you efficiently assess if a platform meets your needs? To ease this burden, we've created a quick guide to Basecamp pricing—which starts at $99 per month for unlimited users. We'll also cover:

- Basecamp cost
- Features
- How it compares to a Basecamp alternative

BASECAMP PRICING PLANS

How much does Basecamp cost? Basecamp offers two plans: Basecamp Personal and Basecamp Business. You can access Basecamp Business for free with a 30-day trial that has anytime cancellation and doesn't require a credit card. Here's a quick breakdown of the plans pricing:

- Basecamp Personal: $0 free plan
- Basecamp Business: $99 per month flat rate

Basecamp's pricing site also offers a 15% discount if you pay for a year subscription up front. It's also worth noting that Basecamp's pricing is not charged based on how many users you have—the price is uniform. While the flat Basecamp cost could be beneficial for large teams, it also means smaller teams might spend more than they really should.

Stick with us, we're about to give you all the details about these Basecamp plans based on their features.

WHAT'S INCLUDED IN BASECAMP PRICING PLANS?

Basecamp pricing plans come with some attractive offerings, like storage space, project templates, and a Company HQ— but it will depend on what you chip in. Before you search, "Is Basecamp free?" check out some of the features for each plan.

Basecamp's free plan is recommended for personal projects, students, freelancers, families, and "light use". The features seem to live up to that last description:

- 3 project maximum
- 20 users
- 1 GB storage space

You wouldn't want to go for this one if you have multiple teams, or plan to work with heavy media and files—you'd really feel the restrictions. To play the devil's advocate, if your team mostly uploads word documents and other file formats with a small footprint, it could be okay.

Companies that handle video editing for example, however, will hit the wall quickly. For context, 4K video takes up a gigabyte of storage for every minute of footage if you're filming at 30 frames per second.

Business

Basecamp Business offers unlimited projects and users. With it, you also get:

- Client access
- 500 GB storage space
- Real-time chat
- To-do lists and schedules

Sounds pretty good, right? Well upon deeper review and verified user research, we can see there is a little bit more to the story—but more on that later in our Basecamp alternative section.

Basecamp alternative

To put Basecamp's price and features in context, let's take a look at how it compares to another project management software out there—monday.com Work OS.

What is monday.com?

monday.com is a Work Operating System (Work OS) anyone and any team can track, and manage projects in their own way—from managing reporting and workloads to resource management and beyond, all while automating manual work. More than 127,000 customers trust our scalable and flexible solution to drive impact for their organizations while helping them pivot and scale according to shifting needs, champion transparency, and work the way they want.

monday.com pricing for 3 seats works like this:

- Individual plan: FREE
- Basic: $8 seat/month
- Standard: $10 seat/month
- Pro: $16 seat/month
- Enterprise: Our consulting team is happy to help you assess your best fit

Visit our pricing page to experiment with the different options to find the right price and solution for your needs.

Free

Our Individual Plan is great for individuals and small teams looking to tackle simple tasks and improve their personal productivity. Enjoy the most essential features of monday.com to develop strong project management skills with:

- monday workdocs as your new go-to doc creator
- A user-friendly search function to navigate your boards with ease
- Unique views: Kanban, File, and Forms
- Extensive apps marketplace

Basic

The Basic plan provides you with the bones to centralize your team's work in one connected platform:

- Unlimited docs, free viewers, and boards
- 20+ column types to get as creative as you want
- A dashboard view
- monday mobile app for Apple and Android devices
- A Template Center with 200+ unique templates

Standard

Standard is our most popular plan and builds upon the features of the Basic plan so you can benefit from advanced search functions, new Calendar and Timeline views, and board sharing with stakeholders. Building and managing your custom work processes is easier than ever with:

- 250 automation actions per month
- 250 integration actions per month
- Dashboards with data from up to 5 boards

Here's what one customer said about our easy adoption on G2:

- "More intuitive and streamlined than Basecamp...monday.com could be a better choice for teams who are not as experienced with using software for project management."

The more complex operations you have, the more you need to streamline—Our Pro plan is fully-equipped to help you do it. Here's what you get inside Pro (in addition to the features included in Basic and Standard):

- 25,000 actions/month each for integrations and automations
- Time-tracking
- Formula and dependency columns
- Private boards and settings
- Up to 10 boards per dashboard

Like Basecamp, monday.com has an Enterprise plan available for large organizations that require enterprise-grade project management security and effective solutions. Enterprise comes with all features from the other plans, plus:

- Enterprise-grade governance & security
- Even more automations and integrations
- Advanced analytics and reporting
- Multi-level permissions
- The monday.com tailored onboarding process
- Up to 50 boards per dashboard
- Priority support

Every plan comes with a 14-day free trial so you can try it out before you buy it.

monday.com vs. Basecamp: how do their features compare?

The need for add-ons

Basecamp brands itself as a complete project management tool kit, for onsite and remote teams. However, this is a little misleading. While you can find classic features including schedules and file storage as well as a unique group chat, many of the features teams want will require purchasing additional add-ons or integrations.

In contrast, most monday.com features are included in our Work OS, such as the ability to create your own connected forms or create and collaborate on documents with monday workdocs.

Basecamp's project visualization is centered mostly around to-do lists and something they call the Hill Chart—while unique to their platform, it creates limitations and might lend itself to blindspots. Hill Charts can be pretty subjective, based entirely on how a specific person feels as they progress through a project.

monday.com is an excellent Basecamp alternative because you have more ways to accurately visualize your projects, from the moment your plan starts to when you want to visualize data at the end. Our Work OS has so many different ways to see your work, including Dashboards or Charts and Calendar, Workload, Timeline, Table, Kanban, Form, and Cards views. The best part is that you can easily toggle between these views and the main board, and save custom views without disrupting others' work.

monday.com is a versatile Basecamp because you can easily create unique workflows and replicate them to be used over and over again in different ways. monday.com has a huge variety of applications — you can use it as:

- A sales CRM
- A video production planning tool
- Document management system
- IT tickets repository
- Performance analysis tool

We have 200+ templates to get started quickly and enjoy more than 40 integrations. To get started, check out how you can streamline your development workflow with monday.com and our Jira integration.

Basecamp offers bot-free customer support with a claim to get back to customers in "about 2 hours". You can watch tutorials, read their help guides, or send them a message via a request form on their support site.

monday.com has 24/7 support via email and our Help Desk year-round. In addition to our support, we also have a knowledge center and YouTube channel full of useful tutorials and new feature updates.

It's easy to get distracted by a flashy price offering or ads for Basecamp pricing. But above all, you have to consider your team's needs right now, and which tool will be able to support them as they change along with your team size and functions.

We recommend you try monday.com, the first two weeks are on us.

ASANA VS. BASECAMP: AN OVERVIEW

Who is Asana for?

Asana was founded in 2008 by Facebook co-founder Dustin Moskovitz and ex-Google engineer Justin Rosenstein with the purpose of "simplifying team-based work management." While this project management tool was later to the game than Basecamp, Asana has been met with critical acclaim thanks to its design and ease of use.

Asana officially launched in 2011, and since then, it has continued to add new features and functions to the platform, including a mobile app, kanban board project management, integrations with outside programs, and project timelines.

When I originally wrote this comparison, I remarked on the lack of any reporting or budgeting features, which, just like Basecamp, made it hard to recommend this tool outside of a narrow collaborative setting.

After re-reviewing Asana in 2020, I was pleased to find that reporting features are now offered, albeit only with the Premium pricing tier. This puts Asana a step above a basic collaboration tool, but it still remains a great option for smaller teams.

Who is Basecamp for?

Basecamp, originally known as 37signals, was launched in 2004 as a web-based project management tool as well as a private American web application development company named after its most successful tool.

The creators of Basecamp wanted to build a project management tool that was simple and straightforward for all businesses to use, from large multinational corporations and small and medium sized businesses to individual freelancers.

Today, we are using their latest iteration, Basecamp 3, which takes everything we love about Basecamp and adds new features that weren't available before, such as group chats, messages, and document storage.

Asana vs. Basecamp: Features

While Asana and Basecamp appeal to similar markets, their features and functions are vastly different. Find out what makes them different and which platform better suits your needs.

What Asana offers

Just like Basecamp, Asana is a collaboration tool first and foremost, and it offers users some variety when it comes to task scheduling, tracking, and completion.

Asana doesn't offer any budgeting or in-depth reporting, but it does provide multiple task tracking options besides simple task lists, including a shared team calendar and Gantt timeline charts. These are welcome additions for those who prefer visual task management over written lists.

Asana truly separates itself with its unique features, such as the Workload management tool. Using this function, you can track the workload of each team member and set limits to how many tasks they can take on at one time in order to prevent burnouts. This kind of automated management makes Asana more of a worker-focused tool rather than just a management platform.

These worker-centric features and flexible task management options elevate Asana above the average checklist-and-chat software. However, Asana does miss the mark on a few key project management features.

As I previously mentioned, there are no native budgeting tools or invoicing/billing options, making Asana more of a collaborative project tool. Hopefully, if the company's development team adds more of these options in the future, Asana will maintain the same level of simplicity and convenience.

When I originally wrote my review for Asana (and subsequent comparison of these two tools), there weren't any reporting features available. As of 2020, Asana made a 180-degree turn in the reporting department by adding these features and executing them in an exceptionally accessible manner.

Using these reporting features, you can track task completion, overdue tasks, and overall project completion. While Asana doesn't offer any native budgeting features for tracking in your reports, it's possible to create report widgets through integrations with other tools.

What Basecamp offers

Basecamp is a basic collaboration tool that offers everything you'd need to coordinate and execute project tasks, including task lists, file/document sharing, task comment sections, project forums, automated project check-ins, schedules, and a message board. This tool is built around providing the simplest ways to accomplish project tracking and completion.

Basecamp empty task template

Outside of this, Basecamp is a little scant on features. It doesn't offer any native budget tracking, time-tracking, resource management, or reporting functions. This tool is made for collaboration -- and not much else.

If you're looking to tracking budgets or any other kinds of reporting, you'll have to take advantage of Basecamp's many integrations that help fill in those gaps. The closest you'll come to native functionality in those areas is by attaching spreadsheet files to individual tasks or uploading them to the project file storage area.

As I said in my Basecamp review, this software may not offer a lot, but what it does offer, it does very well.

Results

It's quite easy to pick Asana as the winner, here. Asana takes what Basecamp has to offer and gives users even more variety in how projects are tracked and managed. Think of Basecamp as a base model car with window cranks, while Asana is the upscale trim with powered seats, a touchscreen infotainment system, and a backup camera.

Asana vs. Basecamp: Support

When it comes to customer support, Basecamp and Asana offer similar types of user guides and troubleshooting help. However, one platform surpasses the other in response time.

What Asana offers

Asana is very similar to Basecamp in the support department. I had a hard time finding a phone number to get in touch with Asana's support team, instead finding only a contact form.

Luckily, Asana offers help guides, FAQs, forums, webinars, and use cases to help you find and solve any issue with the platform. When contacting Asana support through its form, I found its response time a little slow. It took a whole day for someone at Asana to get back to me about a billing issue I was having with the product.

What Basecamp offers

When it comes to customer support, Basecamp offers everything you would expect from a software vendor, except phone support. It does offer a contact support form that promises a response in 30 minutes or less, which is helpful; however, that still doesn't replace the convenience of actually speaking to a human being on the phone.

Of course, considering the extensive tutorials and help guides offered by Basecamp, it seems unlikely there would be many scenarios where you would need to contact support for such a simple tool.

I'm declaring Basecamp the winner, here, even though the platforms offer nearly identical levels of support.

Basecamp wins by a hair simply due to its response time: 30 minutes versus an entire day for response time is a significant difference when major issues crop up (however unlikely that may be when using tools as easy as these).

Both platforms answered my questions accurately, but if timeliness is your thing, then Basecamp wins over Asana.

Asana vs. Basecamp: Ease of use

Asana and Basecamp both prioritize ease of use on their platforms, albeit in different ways.

What Asana offers

Asana offers more functionality than Basecamp, which slightly adds to its difficulty. However, the only real hurdle to clear is the additional time spent learning these other features.

Unlike Basecamp's block system, Asana's user interface opts for a traditional setup with a navigation menu on the left, user options in the top right corner, and whatever task you are working on in the center of the screen.

Asana grant timeline chart with 3 sample tasks

Above is the Gantt timeline view in Asana. You can view all of your tasks in either list, timeline, or calendar format, and these options are listed right under the project name.

This user interface is not only very easy to navigate and understand, but it gives you lots of different options to choose from when planning your projects.

When it comes to ease of use, it doesn't get much easier than Basecamp. Everything in the software is clearly labeled and defined in their own blocks, including projects, to-do lists, files/documents, check-ins, schedules, and "campfire" forums.

Basecamp project dashboard with cards for each function of the software

You couldn't get lost in Basecamp if you tried. Part of what makes it so easy to use is the fact that it leaves a lot of complicated features behind, such as billing and invoicing, budgeting, and reporting. Basecamp is a collaboration tool that utilizes the most basic functions you could ask of a project management software.

It doesn't offer Gantt timeline charts, it doesn't measure team workloads, and it won't display your tasks in a kanban board view.

In Basecamp, you create projects, build to-do lists for those projects, upload project materials, schedule tasks, and discuss your progress. That's pretty much it. Basecamp doesn't offer a whole lot, but if this is all you need, you'll be pleased with how easy it functions.

I have to call a tie. At first, it seemed obvious that I would award this section to Basecamp given how intuitive its user interface is. However, even though Asana offers so many more features, it's impressively easy to navigate through them. So, I have to call this one a tie. Great job on both fronts.

Asana vs. Basecamp: Pricing

Basecamp and Asana differ greatly in pricing. One offers an affordable and easily scalable solution, while the other will demand more from your wallet up front.

What Asana offers

Asana falls a little short in the pricing department, which I made clear in my Asana review. While it does offer a free version of its software, the user limit for it is lower than Basecamp's and only offers a fraction of the capabilities the paid versions have. Asana's paid options certainly do add up over time, especially if you choose the Business option, which includes its unique Workload features and integrations.

- Basic -- Free: includes task lists, kanban boards, calendars, app integrations, up to 15 users.
- Premium -- $9.99/user/month with an annual contract: includes all previous features plus timelines, advanced searches, custom field creation, premium Asana Academy content, and admin privileges.

- Business -- $19.99/user/month with an annual contract: includes all previous features plus portfolios, Workload, forms, automatic proofing, and Adobe Creative Cloud integration.
- Enterprise -- Pricing negotiated with the client: includes all previous features plus user provisioning, data exporting, custom branding, and priority support.

That's not to say the paid tiers of Asana aren't worth it, because they are. Just know that if you decide to go with Asana's Premium tier, with only 10 users, you're already meeting the price of Basecamp.

What Basecamp offers

At first glance, you'd be forgiven for thinking Basecamp was expensive. After all, it offers a flat rate of $99 per month, which means each year, you'll spend $1,200 on this software -- and that's not cheap. So, why did I give its pricing an 8 out of 10 in my Basecamp review?

It's very simple: This monthly rate is all-inclusive. No matter how many projects you create, users you add, or clients you include, you'll pay the same price. Not to mention you are also given 500 GB of storage space, project templates, and all of the other features Basecamp has to offer.

The more team members you add to the software, the less you pay per person, which is more than I can say for many other software options.

Also, if you have a smaller collaborative team that doesn't need lots of storage space, Basecamp now offers a free option for up to 20 users and three projects at a time.

The nod goes to Basecamp this time. Although Asana offers more functionality, a lot of that functionality comes in the form of additional task management views, instructional content, and integrations.

Asana's per user, per month pricing structure gets very expensive, very fast, while Basecamp's price stays the same no matter how much you grow. This makes Basecamp's scalability far more affordable.

Asana vs. Basecamp: Integration with other software

Asana and Basecamp both offer plenty of integrations to help you fill in the gaps not covered by their collaboration-focused features.

What Asana offers

Asana offers plenty of app integrations that'll help you manage any aspect of your projects, including some not offered by Asana's core features. Some of these integrations include:

- Adobe Creative Cloud
- Dropbox
- Microsoft Outlook
- Slack
- Google Calendar
- Everhour Reporting

- Trello
- Mailchimp
- And many others

Basecamp also offers tons of different integrations that will likely cover all the needs of your projects, including some functions not offered by the software itself. These integrations include:

- Everhour Reporting
- Hubstaff
- Ganttify
- ScrumDo
- Akita
- Zapier
- Project Buddy
- And many others

However, Basecamp is missing integrations with major programs like Slack, Mailchimp, and Trello, a severe missed opportunity for this software.

Results

Asana might appeal to more users given its ability to integrate with popular software and programs you likely already use. When it comes to integrations, both offer similar third-party partnerships that help with planning, reporting, invoicing, accounting, and asset management.

However, in my view, Asana comes out ahead based on the additional integrations it offers with several well-known and widely used applications, such as Microsoft Outlook, Trello, and Dropbox.

Asana vs. Basecamp: Getting started

Both Asana and Basecamp offer very simple startup processes, and it takes only minutes to get up and running once you visit their sites. However, only one offers a more comprehensive onboarding experience when it comes to getting your team up to speed with your new project management software.

What Asana offers

Asana's onboarding process is quite similar to Basecamp's, but with an extra step. After I visited Asana's website and entered my information into the free trial form, I received an email welcoming me to use the tool.

Asana's onboarding content was a little harder to find on its website than Basecamp's, but what it offers is far more detailed. This is understandable considering the additional functionality Asana offers. Asana's onboarding content consists of guides for getting started, onboarding your team, managing/planning tasks, and use cases to help structure your experience.

What Basecamp offers

Getting started with Basecamp was very simple. There's a button on its main website, in the top right-hand corner, beckoning you to try its product for free. This takes you to a page offering either the 30-day free trial for the full system, or the free limited version of the software.

Once you click on the 30-day free trial button, you'll be prompted to enter your name and your email address, create a password, enter the name of your company, then select your type of project. Once you've entered all of this information, you are taken right to the main dashboard. It's that simple.

If you're looking for onboarding content, Basecamp provides all of that in the "How It Works" section of its website, which gives you a detailed overview of the tool and its features in the form of a video and screenshots paired with descriptions. When I first used Basecamp, I found it so easy to understand and navigate that I never even bothered with the onboarding content.

Results

Asana's the winner, here. While Basecamp's signup process was faster and easier because I didn't have to check my email to gain access to the tool, Asana provided more content to help me get the ball rolling with my projects.

How They Compare: Asana vs. Basecamp

	BASECAMP	ASANA
TASK LISTS	Yes	Yes
GANTT TIMELINE CHARTS		Yes
SHARED TEAM CALENDAR	Yes	Yes

FILE SHARING	Yes	Yes
COMMUNICATION	Yes	Yes
BUDGETING		
TIME TRACKING		Yes
INVOICING		
OUTSIDE INTEGRATIONS	Yes	Yes
RESOURCE MANAGEMENT		

Which software is the winner?

Based on the scores, Basecamp is the winner; however, you should always take your specific needs into consideration.

While Asana offers more features, more integrations, and a better, more informative startup process, Basecamp offers better pricing and faster support. When it comes to ease of use, both tools are simple, intuitive, and effortless to navigate.

It all comes down to what kind of collaborative experience you're looking for.

If you're looking to scale your team in a simple task management environment without incurring additional costs or user limitations, then Basecamp is probably best for you. If you're looking for additional features and want to get more detailed with tracking your team workload, then Asana is the tool you're looking for.

Basecamp's strengths lie in its simplicity. Navigating to different projects and teams is a breeze on the home screen, with each project and team displayed in giant blocks listed in alphabetical order. I never felt lost while using Basecamp.

If you're looking for a collaboration tool that you can pick up quickly with minimal training or experience with project-management tools, Basecamp is the way to go.

The user-friendly platform is also easy to scale thanks to the flat $99 per month pricing structure. No matter how many projects you create, users you add to the platform, or features you take on, you'll always pay the same rate, making it the ideal collaboration tool for large project teams.

Basecamp's pricing

Basecamp is $99 per month with no contractual obligations, no user limits, and no tiers for features or customer support. This is perfect for teams looking to scale with lots of users without taking on any extra costs. This price may seem relatively expensive right out of the gate, but the more users you bring on, the more economical it gets.

Additionally, Basecamp has added a free version of its software for freelancers, students, families, and personal project needs. This version, named Basecamp Personal, offers users the ability to create three projects, add twenty users, and use up to 1GB of storage space. This free tier is perfect for entry-level users looking to test the waters before upgrading to the full platform!Usability

When it comes to usability, you can't get much easier than Basecamp. Everything is clearly labeled with large project icons on the dashboard, and each project clearly lays out your message board, to-do list, automatic check-ins, schedule, "campfire" discussion feature, and file/document uploads. If your project doesn't involve handling money or outside contractors, what more could you want in a collaboration tool?

Basecamp's file upload system makes the ideation process simple and convenient. If I need feedback on a graphic, an email, or a social campaign, all I have to do is upload my ideas into a task and tag the relevant team members to let them know. Once tagged, those users will receive an email letting them know that I've pinged them in case they aren't currently on Basecamp. If I need to create tasks, it's as easy as clicking into a project, entering the "to-dos" section, and adding a new task with a due date and the relevant users.

Furthermore, Basecamp even offers a mobile app so you can keep in contact with your team on the go. I found that the mobile app functions almost exactly like the desktop version. The icons look nearly identical, the comment functions are the same, and the team pinging functions are intuitive, with notification bubbles at the top of the home screen.

Easy, easy, easy.

Basecamp doesn't offer everything you could ever want in a project management software, but what it does offer, it does very well.

Is there a free version of Basecamp?

Basecamp has recently released a new free version of its software named "Basecamp Personal." This free option is quite generous with a creation limit of three separate projects at one time, twenty user limit, and 1 GB of storage space. They advertise this option as a great choice for personal projects, cash strapped students, freelancers, and families.

I see this option as a fantastic choice for users looking to test out Basecamp before committing to the paid version which removes the limits on projects and users while upping the storage space to 500 GB.

What kinds of teams and projects work best with Basecamp?

Basecamp is best for internal project teams that don't require tracking expenditures or external invoices with contractors or other outside actors. This system is best for increasing collaboration between internal teams and tracking the progress of their tasks.

I've found Basecamp works very well with creative projects that require lots of input from different team members. For anything outside of collaborating and tracking tasks, you might want to look to a more comprehensive project management tool.

3 KEY BENEFITS OF BASECAMP PROJECT MANAGEMENT

Now that we've covered four delicious Basecamp features, we're gonna add some cherries on top. Not one, not two, but three!

Here are three great benefits of using Basecamp for project management:

1. Helps you organize project files in one place

Managing multiple projects and keeping track of project data is no easy task. From project plans and charters to scope of work documents, there's just a lot to juggle. Fortunately, Basecamp's document management and file storage features can help you out here. Each project has a separate doc and file sharing section to ensure everything is organized correctly. You can track each file's version history and even use a color-coded system for better file storage management. This way, your team members can be on the same page (literally!) and avoid making things complicated.

2. Built-in chat features for streamlined communication

Sometimes you just need a quick reply. With Basecamp's built-in chat feature, Campfire, your teams can discuss anything they want and get answers instantly. It's just like having a quick chat around a campfire!

Some people like extra mayo in their sandwiches, while others prefer honey mustard. Anyway, it goes without saying that the same applies to workplace software. Recognizing the power of different tastes, Basecamp lets you integrate the app with other popular tools.

You can choose from apps for time tracking, reporting, client relationship management, and more. This way, you can keep all your favorite apps and streamline processes across them.

CHAPTER TWO

BASECAMP 3 PROJECT MANAGEMENT: EVERYTHING YOU NEED TO KNOW

Basecamp 3 is the latest iteration of the popular project management software, and it comes with a whole raft of improvements from Basecamp 2 that have the potential to revolutionize the way that you work.

David Heinemeir Hansson, the creator of Ruby on Rails and founder and CTO of Basecamp, described the creation of Basecamp 3 as being like building a Porsche 911, and when you start to compare different versions you can see why.

Basecamp 3 is a project management machine, reimagined from the ground up with a whole heap of new features that are designed to make it as functional – and as easy to use – as possible. It's the little details that count, and Basecamp 3 has them all – including such nifty features as the ability to limit notifications to working hours and to schedule automated check-ins.

When you put all of this together you get one of the most effective project management tools on the market. We swear by it, which is why we've pulled together our best advice to help you to make the most of it.

Is Basecamp 3 for Me?

The short answer is 'probably, yes.' Here's the long answer.

Like any piece of project management Basecamp software, Basecamp 3 has its pros and cons. It's not perfect because nothing ever is, and while the latest build includes a whole heap of new and updated features, it can also lead to a culture shock for people who are used to older versions.

Discover how the system fairs against some of its closest competitors in our quick comparisons to help you get to grips with which is best for you:

- Basecamp Vs. Trello – See how Basecamp measures up when compared to the popular project management system Trello. Everhour also has Trello time tracking integration on board
- Basecamp Vs. Asana – Learn about the disadvantages and advantages of both Asana and Basecamp and find out which one meets your business's needs.

Like any business tool, Basecamp 3 is only as good as the people that use it. Employee uptake will determine its success, and if they fail to take full advantage of its features or to keep projects fully updated, your implementation of the software is doomed to failure.

In fact, most complaints about Basecamp 3 are actually down to human error. Some say that it's difficult to find information or that there are too many updates to keep up with, but both of these can be combatted by a concentrated effort to keep the software as well-organized and as up-to-date as possible.

Basecamp 3 isn't for everyone but used correctly it can level up your project management to the point at which the added efficiency pays for the software. This is often a key argument for smaller businesses who want to use the software but who worry that they don't deal with enough projects to justify the cost of a license.

Luckily, discounts are available if you pay yearly (you'll save 15%), and Basecamp is free for teachers and students and half the price for charities and non-profits. There's also a free trial on offer so you can try before you buy and, at just $99/month for unlimited users and unlimited projects, it's usually worth the investment for bigger businesses.

Getting Started with Basecamp 3

The good news is that it doesn't take long to get started with the latest iteration of basecamp. The software offers its own onboarding process to guide new users through the interface, and it typically takes less than half an hour to get the basics in place and to send out invites to team members.

But before you invite people to join your projects, you'll want to make sure that Basecamp is already set up with all of the information that employees are likely to need. To do it properly, you'll need to take advantage of Basecamp's tiered approach:

- HQ: For company-wide communication
- Teams: For specific teams to work together

- Projects: Individual projects that are assigned to specific teams

Make sure that you arrange your work to fit within this hierarchy so that your Basecamp 3 setup has a logical structure that fits within the constraints of the software. Pay particular attention to projects and make sure that you're not simply listing tasks that would work better as part of a to-do list.

Not sure how to tell whether something's a project or a task for the to-do list? Projects are usually at a larger scale and include multiple tasks, while tasks are little tweaks and fixes. "Redesign the website" is a project. "Add social networking links" is a task.

Basecamp 3: Tools for Project Management

Basecamp 3 is full to the brim of little tools and integrations that you can use to take your project management process to the next level. Many of these are unique to the software, which means you won't be able to get them from a competitor.

At its most basic level, Basecamp includes six core tools that can be used at all levels of the software, from HQ level right down to teams and individual projects. Here's a list of what they are and what they're good for.

To-Dos

Good For: Tracking tasks and assigning priorities

Basecamp 3 has rethought the way that to-dos work to make them more powerful than ever. Designed to break larger projects up into smaller, bite-sized chunks, to-do lists are easy to set up and highly customizable.

You can add details for each item using a visual text editor, and Basecamp makes it easy for you to assign them to users and to set a deadline. Users will receive automated reminders whenever they're added to a to-do list or when a deadline is due, making it an easy way to manage the day-to-day tasks that your department is working on.

Pro Tip: You can move items around (and between lists) by dragging the small icon to the left. You can also drag and drop entire lists when needed.

Message Board

Good For: Sharing announcements, updates, and key communication

The message board in Basecamp 3 is one of two tools that are specifically designed to foster internal communication.

The message board is the more formal of the two, designed to pull together conversations around a single topic and to cut down on emails. No more CCing and forwarding old emails to new employees – with Basecamp 3, you can do it all within the interface. You can even import external emails and discuss them with your team before replying to the original sender.

Pro Tip: Encourage employees to check their "Hey!" menu every time they log into Basecamp. This menu is "a single inbox for nearly every kind of Basecamp notification", and it pulls together everything from new messages to @mentions, assignments, and project progress.

Campfires

Good For: Casual chat and quick discussions

If the message board is the equivalent of a sit-down meeting then campfires are like gathering around the water cooler. This group chat functionality is built-in at the center of every Basecamp and is designed for quick communication without any fuss, offering a more ephemeral alternative to the more formal message boards.

Pro Tip: Used correctly, campfires can replace existing instant-messaging tools. Alternatively, if you're already using Slack or something similar then be sure to check whether Basecamp offers integration. It supports 50+ market-leading applications and can help to centralize information in a single place.

Schedule

Good For: Tracking progress, deadlines, and milestones

The schedule does exactly what its name suggests. Tapping into the project and task list data that you've added to the system, it will update itself in real-time to show you milestones, deadlines, and more so you know what you're working on and when it needs to be completed. You can discuss your schedule from within the application and export the data to your Google, iCal, or Outlook calendars.

Pro Tip: Basecamp 3 has a nifty piece of functionality that allows you to set your working hours. That way, you won't receive emails or notifications in the evenings or at weekends. But don't worry – everything will be waiting for you when you return to the office!

Docs & Files

Good For: Storing and sorting assets

Forget Dropbox. Basecamp 3 includes a stunning document storage system that helps you to organize all of the files that you need to get the work done. The system also allows users to color-code files to make it easier to discover them, and the powerful search functionality means you'll never lose sight of your files again.

Pro Tip: Integrate Basecamp 3 with Google Docs to bring together files from disparate places, and be sure to create a folder structure that groups similar files together for ease of use.

Automatic Check-ins

Good For: Getting updates without having to hassle people

Imagine if you could automate the process of asking staff for progress updates. Well, thanks to Basecamp 3, now you can. The new automatic check-ins feature allows you to specify what to ask, who to ask and when to ask it. Then it will gather the responses and forward them over in an easy-to-read report. The good thing about this tool is that it becomes exponentially more powerful as your company grows, and the smart use of automation can save time and money while improving morale across the company.

Pro Tip: Think outside the box. Don't just ask, "How are you?" Ask for feedback on specific projects or set up check-in on Friday that asks employees for their thoughts on the coming week. When you get the feedback, act on it – otherwise, you send out the message that responding to check-ins is a waste of time.

Basecamp 3: Tips for Pro Users

By now, you should have seen enough evidence to prove that Basecamp 3 is one of the best project management tools on the market. In fact, this latest iteration is so feature-rich that no article could ever hope to list every single thing you can use it for.

That said, we still have a few more tips up our sleeve. Here are a few final tricks to try out once you've got your head around the basics.

Take advantage of integrations

Use Basecamp's bank of integrations to upgrade functionality, such as by bringing in time tracking, estimates, and reporting. Everhour natively integrates into your Basecamp interface so your employees' workflow stays pretty much the same. That's important because it minimizes the learning curve of your team.

Use Clientside

Clientside is specifically designed to create a sanitized version of your Basecamp account to share with clients, freelancers, and suppliers. It allows you to keep discussions with your team and discussions with your client completely separate, and it'll also store all of the feedback that you receive in a single place.

Customize your toolbox

Too much choice can be counterproductive, which is why Basecamp 3 makes it easy for you to turn tools on and off by team or by the project. Disable tools if you're not using them to streamline your use of the software.

Use bookmarks

Set up bookmarks for your favorite files so that you don't waste time looking for them over and over again. Your bookmarks will also synchronize between devices so that they're always on hand.

Keep an eye on your timeline

This useful little feature is at the bottom of every Basecamp and shows everything that's happened since the start of a project. If you're looking for something, it's a good bet that you'll be able to find it here.

Use reports

Basecamp 3 allows you to generate real-time reports that show everything from individual employee work records to project progress and an overall timeline and work schedule.

Notifications are one of Basecamp 3's most useful – and most well-thought-out – features. They're designed to reach you where you are, so they'll try a desktop notification if you're logged in at your machine and follow it with mobile or email notifications if you're not around.

If you don't want to use Clientside but you still want to share something, you can selectively share with outsiders by hitting the share button and choosing the 'public link' option.

THE ULTIMATE BEGINNER'S GUIDE TO BASECAMP

Do you remember the game telephone? You'd relay a message down a line of kids by whispering to the person next to you, and by the end the message would be completely different from the start. If this is how your projects feel at work, you might want to consider using Basecamp.

Basecamp is a work management and collaboration tool that helps you organize projects and communications. It's benefits are clear: it keeps you and your work organized, making it clear what tasks are due and gathering all the information you need to execute on them; it brings everyone in your team and company onto the same page, allowing you to communicate more efficiently in a single place; and it allows you to maintain control over projects while easily sharing specific information and deliverables with clients.

If you're just getting started with the tool, this beginner's guide to Basecamp will help you spend more time getting stuff done and less time trying to sort out the moving pieces.

Continue reading to learn more about:

- The different parts of your Basecamp dashboard
- Key Basecamp features you need to know to get started successfully
- How to create a project in Basecamp

GETTING STARTED WITH BASECAMP

Now that you understand some fundamental ways Basecamp can benefit your business, it's time to get started actually using the tool. We'll start by taking a look at the main areas of the tool, and then show you Basecamp's key features. And if you don't already have an account, you can try Basecamp for free for 30 days.

The Basecamp dashboard

Basecamp gives you three ways to organize projects and stay on top of whatever's going on with your clients and team. These are: the HQ, Teams, and Projects.

HQ

When you first log in to Basecamp, you'll land on the HQ (Headquarters) first. This is automatically set up once you create your account. It's recommended that you invite everybody in your company to the HQ so they can all see relevant message board posts, company-wide announcements, and documents like the holiday calendar or technology-usage policies.

Teams

The Teams section is where you can organize people in the company by department or role. This create a hub where team members can share important information, announcements, updates, or participate in chats — saving time and making teams more efficient. In this hub team members can also keep track of items on the to-do list and project schedules, and find assets they need in the reference materials portal.

Projects

The Projects section is the final component on your Basecamp home page. This is where individuals with different roles can come together for the purpose of projects (like for a multidisciplinary squad). This lets all the people who are working on a specific project share tasks, timelines, and files. It also allows teams to message each other, ease communication and stay aligned until the project's completion.

The menu bar at the top of your page will stay with you as you navigate Basecamp. It lets you easily review account activity and find whatever you need no matter what page or section you're on.

Home

The home button (shaped like a tent) will take you back to your main home page whenever you need to see your HQ, Teams, or Projects sections.

Pings

Pings are direct messages and conversations with other users in the account. They don't need to be tied to any Teams or Projects assignments.

Hey!

The Hey! button will alert you to any notifications from any workspace (Teams, Projects, HQ) you're connected to. If you see an orange badge next to your Hey! button, you have a notification.

Activity

The Activity button will show you all of the, you guessed it, activity on your account. This means you'll see any to-dos, late assignments (oopsies), upcoming deadlines, and other assignment information and reports.

Find

Use this button to search for anything in your Basecamp account. Search for a project component completed by a certain teammate, a logo you really need for a client package, or anything else that lives in Basecamp.

KEY BASECAMP FEATURES YOU NEED TO KNOW

Once you're aware of the basic components of Basecamp, you can get familiar with the key features that will quickly become second nature.

To-dos

To-do lists might seem like a basic way of keeping track of what needs to get done, but that's why they work so well. Listing your personal tasks or your team's tasks where everyone can see them helps not only clear your mind and organize priorities, but gives everyone visual goals and next steps.

In Basecamp, you can assign items on to-do lists to one or more people, add notes and files, comment, and track work.

Campfire

When you don't want to start a thread or post a message, Campfire lets you chat in real-time. This is great for quick questions, and is especially handy if you or your company don't have a separate chat app like Slack.

Every Project, Team, and HQ has its own Campfire room, making it extra helpful for organizing communication.

Message boards

The Message Boards tool is helpful when you have a piece of content like a team announcement or big project update that needs to be seen by everyone on a Team or Project and requires a more permanent home. You can take your organization to the next level and categorize messages posted to the Message Board (ie. Announcement, Question, etc.), along with leave comments or reactions to other users' posts.

Schedule

A project without a schedule is basically just a dream. Thankfully, every project in Basecamp has a dedicated schedule where everyone can see what's coming up, what's past due, and what's been successfully completed.

Automatic check-ins

Find yourself closer to inbox zero than ever before. Basecamp's automatic check-ins feature lets you create recurring questions that will be sent to your team on a regular basis of your choosing. For example, you could schedule an automatic check-in question like "What is your top priority this week?" or "What is your biggest blocker this week?" to be sent out to your team every Monday morning. Responses are visible to everyone, so you could also include more casual and friendly questions that will let teammates get to know each other better.

Docs and files

Sometimes just trying to find the right file or hunt down a document can take more time than the work itself. The Docs & Files feature in Basecamp gives your team one set location to upload (with easy drag and drop), store, and access key files for every project. Every file includes a complete version history (say goodbye to millions of documents titled V1 to V15) and you can color code to your Type-A heart's content.

While there are a ton of other features to discover in Basecamp, digging into these features will have you and your team more organized in no time.

Now that you have an understanding of the benefits and elements of Basecamp, it's time to apply this knowledge. If you want to organize a project in basecamp, follow these simple steps:

1. Go to your homepage and scroll down to where the "Projects" heading is. Click the "New" button with the green plus sign.

2. Name your project. You might want to use your client's name or another name that everyone involved with can easily recognize.

3. Once you've created the project, it will appear in your Projects section.

4. Start adding the appropriate people to the project by clicking on the "Invite some people" button.

5. At this point, you'll want to add important milestones, events, meetings, and deadlines to the calendar. Click on the 'Schedule' section to start.

6. Once you see the calendar, click on the green 'New event' button and enter the appropriate details.

7. You can also set some To-dos to align with your calendar entries. Click on the 'To-dos' button on the project page and create your to-do list. Once this is created, you can assign items to certain people and check tasks off as they're completed.

8. The rest of your project setup follows the same format. From your project homepage, you can start a Campfire discussion, post key information to the Message Board, and start uploading any relevant documents to the Docs & Files area. If you need help with any of these tasks, Basecamp has a simple help tool that is standing by.

That's all there is to it. Basecamp is known to be one of the easiest solutions for project management. Try it out and see if it works for you.

Pro tip: Using Basecamp like a pro

Learning how to use the tool is just the first step. Next, you need to start thinking like a pro. Basecamp pros make sure to limit the number of notifications they get, use emojis to communicate things quickly, and use project updates liberally. That's just the tip of the iceberg, though.

How to integrate Basecamp with other tools

Learning how to use Basecamp is great, but what about slotting it in with your tool stack? Without the right integration, you can spend hours just copying and pasting information from tool to tool so everyone's in the loop. Just because a tool is great for your needs doesn't mean it works for another team. No one should be forced to use a tool that doesn't fit their workflow.

Want to save time and effort? Try Unito. Unito has the deepest two-way integrations for some of the most popular tools on the market, including Basecamp, Asana, Trello, Google Sheets, and more.

Sync data across tools seamlessly, use rules to filter out irrelevant information, and map fields so everything ends up exactly where it needs to go. All of that in just a few minutes.

Basecamp is an online tool for simple project management. We've used Basecamp for over 3 years to manage projects at SpinWeb. Here are some tips we've picked up along the way:

1. Basecamp is for the Team. For over 2 years, we followed an "Everything in Basecamp" mantra. All emails to clients came from Basecamp. Clients could see todos & milestones. We found is that Basecamp is great for tracking tasks, delegating, and communicating with your team. We found out that clients didn't really care to see the details. They were asking for the big picture; not the behind the scenes tour.

2. Email is for clients. Out of 80+ clients who had a project managed in Basecamp, only 3 of them played by the rules we set up. The rest would forget passwords, email us directly, or just get frustrated. Basecamp emails creeped them out. Training them on how to understand Basecamp didn't help. They just wanted a website, not learning how to communicate by our rules.

3. Be Inbox Zero. Now we keep our communication with clients in simple emails. Using Inbox Zero for email management, it's easy to find the last

reply, CC anyone who needs to know and get things communicated. I don't even have client folders (GASP!). Learn client's names; then use the search tools in your email to find the last email to / from them. It's super easy.

4. Maximize Project Templates. This is a newer feature and is the best time-saver I've found. We have a system that all of projects follow, but now I can create to-do lists, milestones, and link them together before a project is even created. You can also default which members of your company are on a project template. It's awesome-sauce.

5. Use Active, On Hold, Archive. This helpful setting gets me into trouble. When used well, it keeps the Active projects at the top of the list. On Hold projects are grayed out and down at the bottom of your dashboard. The problem is that On Hold projects don't show up on the dashboard, so they can be easy to miss if you assign tasks/milestones and forget to make the project Active again. Archive is great, it puts the projects on a totally different page and hides them away so you don't cry when you see that project that didn't go so well years ago.

6. Subscribe to Project Updates via Email. The lack of project updates from Basecamp is the area that's almost a deal-breaker for me. As project manager, I like to know when things get checked off - or when they haven't been worked on. This feature sends me an email each morning when something

happens in the previous 24 hours. It shows me any new or checked off items. Mostly, it gives me a ping to click the project link and take a peak at what happened the day before. It works OK, but not ideal.

7. Hack the companies. Once we purged the clients out of Basecamp, we realized that "Companies" are the secret for organizing projects by phase. We had struggled with this for over 2 years, since Basecamp likes to organize projects alphabetically by Company. You can still use client companies if you need to, but the follow will help you organize projects the way you want to see them.

How to Organize the Dashboard by Phase:

This tip uses the little known "File under this company" drop down (Well - I was ignoring it for years). This gives you a list of all the companies you've added to a project on under "People & Permissions". This is handy for organizing a project that has multiple companies on it.

First, create a number scheme of how many phases your projects have. Here's mine:

- [1.1 First Phase]
- [1.2 Next part of that phase, if it needs to be tracked]
- [2.1 Second Phase]

The numbers don't really matter, so long as they are sequential. This makes the phases in order when

Basecamp alphabetizes them on the dashboard. I added brackets to the names; it just looked better to me. Add these companies from the Dashboard > "All People".

As of now, you can't automatically add your project phase/companies via a Project Template (only your company/people). This is a shame, but it takes 2 minutes to add them all when you setup a project. This time is well spent getting things setup at the start.

Now, when a project moves from phase to phase, simply change which Company it's filed under on the "Project Settings" tab. Your new dashboard will list out each phase, with the project names underneath. Pretty cool, huh?

UPDATE 2/1/2010: Maximize Project Templates:

The "Hack the Companies" tip works well when Basecamp is accessed primarily from the web interface, often in a desktop environment. Unfortunately, it's not so friendly for Basecamp Extras & Add-ons mobile apps or 3rd party applications like ProofHQ.com (SpinWeb uses it to colloborate with our Web Designers for design revisions). In this case it's best to use the traditional company setup for clients, with micro sub-projects for project phases. At the request of a few team mobile workers, I changed our system to focus on project phases.

1. Setup Project Templates for phases. At SpinWeb, we split our projects into 5 phases (Blueprint, Design, Deploy, Build, Launch). Each phase is

independant with it's own timeframes (Building a site doesn't start until the Design is approved).

2. Sliding milestones. Separating project phases is great for using the built in "Shift future milestones too?" feature. Start with the first milestone in the series, and you can move the whole gang with a few clicks!

3. Space your milestones in advance. The best feature of a Template is that you setup Milestones, To-do lists, and assignments in advance. Use the sidebar calendar grid to see how your timeframes stack up.

4. Link your To-do lists to the Milestones.

Within a few minutes, you can have a pre-populated project that use your best practices. Update your template often to keep improving each new project.

Advanced Basecamp Tips and Tricks for Pros

Many of Basecamp users are digital firms, marketing agencies, and professional services organizations. In fact, the PM tool has features geared for clients that make it easy to work with multiple projects from multiple customers.

1. Flip the Switch

Anything that users on Basecamp 3 can do with their team, they can also do with their clients. They can assign to-dos, share files and folders, chat, and more. However, everything in a project starts off as private only with the team. Once the user is ready to make the project visible to clients, they can simply click a setting to allow visibility to their clients.

2. Create a Template

Basecamp 3 allows users to create templates for work that they do over and over. For instance, they can create Schedule templates and To-do templates with dates relative to the start of their project. They can also manage them to view, edit, archive or delete. Users can even rename the tools that come with every project, or toggle them on or off.

3. Read the Reports

Everything that the team enters will be available in reports. For instance, information includes all the latest activity, overdue to-dos, upcoming dates, to-dos added and completed, and more. A special type of report is the Hill Chart. As a matter of fact, Basecamp itself uses Hill Charts to track the progress of their to-do lists.

4. Customize Notifications

Basecamp 3 provides users some flexibility in how they want to be notified with work. For example, the Hey! menu is the nexus of all notifications. In addition, they have the option to get email notification also. They can temporarily disable them all, or set the hours that a user can be notified only. The use of @mention will also trigger a notification.

Basecamp has a good number of integrations with other productivity tools. Generally, they range from mobile and desktop apps, time tracking, invoicing, charts, reporting, and exporting tools. For a great reporting and exporting tool for Basecamp, we recommend you use our own tool Bridge24 for Basecamp.

CONCLUSION

Basecamp takes all of the core necessities of project collaboration and offers them for a simple flat price, no matter which features you use, number of users you have, or support you need. This product is perfect for large collaborative teams looking to scale without breaking the bank. However, Basecamp is lacking if you're looking for a comprehensive project management software with budgeting, time tracking, and invoicing features.

Basecamp is a platform designed to help you manage work by breaking it up into separate projects. Projects contain everything related to people, discussions, dates, tasks, and files.

With so many of testimonials for this tool, it surely is one of the best project management tools in place till now. Although some other tools are catching up for sure, Basecamp remains the favorite among many users because it's super easy on the eyes in terms of visualization. For a manager managing multiple projects, it just looks like the top of the desk neatly arranged! Thus, allowing the manager to just focus on more important things rather than struggling around with managing the top of the desk.